THE 30-MINUTE SHAKESPEARE

A MIDSUMMER
NIGHT'S D

"Nick Newlin's work as a teaching artist for Folger Education during the past thirteen years has provided students, regardless of their experience with Shakespeare or being on stage, a unique opportunity to tread the boards at the Folger Theatre. Working with students to edit Shakespeare's plays for performance at the annual Folger Shakespeare Festivals has enabled students to gain new insights into the Bard's plays, build their skills of comprehension and critical reading, and just plain have fun working collaboratively with their peers.

Folger Education promotes performance-based teaching of Shakespeare's plays, providing students with an interactive approach to Shakespeare's plays in which they participate in a close reading of the text through intellectual, physical, and vocal engagement. Newlin's *The 30-Minute Shakespeare* series is an invaluable resource for teachers of Shakespeare, and for all who are interested in performing the plays."

ROBERT YOUNG, PH.D.
DIRECTOR OF EDUCATION
FOLGER SHAKESPEARE LIBRARY

A Midsummer Night's Dream: The 30-Minute Shakespeare
ISBN 978-1-935550-00-6
Adaptation, essays, and notes © 2010 by Nick Newlin

Cover design by Sarah Juckniess
Printed in the United States of America

Distributed by Consortium Book Sales & Distribution
www.cbsd.com

NICOLO WHIMSEY PRESS
www.nicolowhimsey.com

Art Director: Sarah Juckniess
Managing Editor: Katherine Little

A MIDSUMMER NIGHT'S DREAM

AS HATH BEEN SUNDRY TIMES
PUBLICLY ACTED
by the
LORD CHAMBERLAIN'S MEN

THE 30-MINUTE SHAKESPEARE

Written by WILLIAM SHAKESPEARE

Abridged AND Edited
by NICK NEWLIN

Nicolo Whimsey
Press

Brandywine, MD

To my Mom,
Louisa Newlin
Thanks for the
inspiration and support.

Special thanks to Joanne Flynn, Bill Newlin, Eliza Newlin Carney, William and Louisa Newlin, Michael Tolaydo, Hilary Kacser, Sarah Juckniess, Katherine Little, Eva Zimmerman, Julie Schaper and all of Consortium, Leo Bowman and the students, faculty, and staff at Banneker Academic High School, and Robert Young PhD and the Folger Shakespeare Library, especially the wonderful Education Department.

✳ TABLE OF CONTENTS

✳ NO EXPERIENCE NECESSARY

I was not a big "actor type" in high school, so if you weren't either, or if the young people you work with are not, then this book is for you. Whether or not you work with "actor types," you can use this book to stage a lively and captivating thirty-minute version of a Shakespeare play. No experience is necessary.

When I was about eleven years old, my parents took me to see Shakespeare's *Two Gentlemen of Verona,* which was being performed as a Broadway musical. I didn't comprehend every word I heard, but I was enthralled with the language, the characters, and the story, and I understood enough of it to follow along. From then on, I associated Shakespeare with *fun.*

Of course Shakespeare is fun. The Elizabethan audiences knew it, which is one reason he was so popular. It didn't matter that some of the language eluded them. The characters were passionate and vibrant, and their conflicts were compelling. Young people study Shakespeare in high school, but more often than not they read his work like a text book and then get quizzed on academic elements of the play, such as plot, theme, and vocabulary. These are all very interesting, but not nearly as interesting as standing up and performing a scene! It is through performance that the play comes alive and all its "academic" elements are revealed. There is nothing more satisfying to a student or teacher than the feeling of "owning" a Shakespeare play, and that can only come from performing it.

But Shakespeare's plays are often two or more hours long, making the performance of an entire play almost out of the question. One can perform a single scene, which is certainly a good start, but what about the story? What about the changes a character goes through as the play progresses? When school groups perform one scene unedited, or when they lump several plays together, the audience can get lost. This is why I have always preferred to tell the story of the play.

The 30-Minute Shakespeare gives students and teachers a chance to get up on their feet and act out a Shakespeare play in half an hour, using his language. The emphasis is on key scenes, with narrative bridges between scenes to keep the audience caught up on the action. The stage directions are built into this script so that young actors do not have to stand in one place; they can move and tell the story with their actions as well as their words. And it can all be done in a classroom during class time!

That is where this book was born: not in a research library, a graduate school lecture, a professional stage, or even an after-school drama club. All of the play cuttings in *The 30-Minute Shakespeare* were first rehearsed in a D.C. public high school English class, and performed successfully at the Folger Shakespeare Library's annual Secondary School Shakespeare Festival. The players were not necessarily "actor types." For many of them, this was their first performance in a play.

Something almost miraculous happens when students perform Shakespeare. They "get" it. By occupying the characters and speaking the words out loud, students gain a level of understanding and appreciation that is unachievable by simply reading the text. That is the magic of a performance-based method of learning Shakespeare, and this book makes the formerly daunting task of staging a Shakespeare play possible for anybody.

With *The 30-Minute Shakespeare* book series I hope to help teachers and students produce a Shakespeare play in a short amount of time, thus jump-starting the process of discovering the beauty, magic, and fun of the Bard. Plot, theme, and language reveal themselves through the performance of these half-hour play cuttings, and everybody involved receives the priceless gift of "owning" a piece of Shakespeare. The result is an experience that is fun and engaging, and one that we can all carry with us as we play out our own lives on the stages of the world.

NICK NEWLIN
Brandywine, MD
March 2010

CHARACTERS IN THE PLAY

The following is a list of characters that appear in this cutting.
For the full breakdown of characters, see Sample Program.

THESEUS: Duke of Athens, father to Hermia

HIPPOLYTA: Queen of the Amazons

EGEUS: Father to Hermia

PHILOSTRATE: Master of the Revels to Theseus

HERMIA:

LYSANDER:
⎬ Four Lovers
HELENA:

DEMETRIUS:

OBERON: King of the Fairies

TITANIA: Queen of the Fairies

ROBIN GOODFELLOW (PUCK): A hobgoblin in Oberon's service

PEASBLOSSOM:

COBWEB:
⎬ Fairies attending upon Titania

MUSTARDSEED:

NICK BOTTOM THE WEAVER/PYRAMUS

PETER QUINCE THE CARPENETER/PROLOGUE

TOM SNOUT THE TINKER/WALL

SNUG THE JOINER/LION

ROBIN STARVELING THE TAILOR/MOON

LORDS AND ATTENDANTS ON THESEUS AND HIPPOLYTA

FAIRIES IN THE TRAINS OF TITANIA AND OBERON

✳ SCENE 1 (ACT III, SCENE II).

STAGEHANDS ONE AND TWO *bring bench downstage right and set it at an angle, downstage of pillar.* **STAGEHANDS THREE AND FOUR** *bring bench downstage left and set it at an angle in front of pillar.*

NARRATOR 1 *(walks from rear to downstage center)*

> In the woods outside of Athens, Oberon, the king of the fairies, and Puck, a hobgoblin in Oberon's service are wreaking havoc on the love lives of our characters by anointing their eyes with love juice, sometimes with unexpected consequences!
> > *Exit stage right.*

SOUND OPERATOR *plays* Sound Cue #1 *(New Age music) on boom box.*

FAIRIES *enter from stage rear, waving scarves and wands. They huddle together, giggle loudly, and exit stage rear.*

Another part of the wood. Enter **OBERON** *from rear.*

OBERON

> I wonder if Titania be awaked;
> Then, what it was that next came in her eye,
> Which she must dote on in extremity.-
> Here comes my messenger.
> > *Enter* **PUCK** *stage right, standing up on stage right bench.*

How now, mad spirit!
What night-rule now about this haunted grove?

PUCK (*moving toward* **OBERON** *while still on bench*)
My mistress with a monster is in love.
(*leaps joyously off bench*)
A crew of patches, rude mechanicals,
Were met together to rehearse a play,
The shallowest thickskin of that barren sort,
An ass's nole I fixed on his head:
So, at his sight, away his fellows fly;
When in that moment,—so it came to pass,—
Titania waked, and straightway loved an ass.

OBERON *and* **PUCK** *come together center and high five, look at each other, start laughing, and fall back on benches with their legs kicking up.*

OBERON
This falls out better than I could devise.
But hast thou yet latch'd the Athenian's eyes
With the love-juice, as I did bid thee do?

PUCK
I took him sleeping,—that is finish'd too,—
And the Athenian woman by his side;
That, when he waked, of force she must be eyed.

Enter **HERMIA** *and* **DEMETRIUS** *stage right. He is pursuing her.*

OBERON
Stand close: this is the same Athenian.

PUCK *and* **OBERON** *hide behind stage left pillar to watch.*

PUCK

    This is the woman, but not this the man.

DEMETRIUS

    O, why rebuke you him that loves you so?

HERMIA

    For thou, I fear, hast given me cause to curse.
    If thou hast slain Lysander in his sleep,
    See me no more, whether he be dead or no.
        HERMIA pushes DEMETRIUS *onto stage right bench.*
        Exit stage rear.

DEMETRIUS

    There is no following her in this fierce vein:
    Here therefore for a while I will remain.
        (lies down and sleeps on stage right bench)

OBERON *and* PUCK *tiptoe out from behind pillar to look at* DEMETRIUS, *and then tiptoe toward him. When* OBERON *sees that it is* DEMETRIUS, *he turns slowly towards* PUCK, *angry and annoyed, advancing toward him while* PUCK *retreats step by step until he is backed into stage left bench.*

OBERON

    What hast thou done? thou hast mistaken quite,
    And laid the love-juice on some true-love's sight:
    About the wood go swifter than the wind,
    And Helena of Athens look thou find:
    By some illusion see thou bring her here:
    I'll charm his eyes against she do appear.

PUCK

    I go, I go; look how I go,
        (turns and runs into stage left pillar,

spins around dizzy)
Swifter than arrow from the Tartar's bow.
Exit stage left.

OBERON *(advances toward* **DEMETRIUS***)*
Flower of this purple dye,
Hit with Cupid's archery,
(squeezes the flower on **DEMETRIUS'S** *eyelids)*

SOUND OPERATOR *plays* Sound Cue #2 *("rrrrinng" sound with chimes).*

Sink in apple of his eye!
When his love he doth espy,
Let her shine as gloriously
As the Venus of the sky. *(looks heavenward)*

Enter **PUCK** *from stage rear. He taps* **OBERON** *from behind on the shoulder;* **OBERON** *turns around, doesn't see him, turns back around, then laughs upon seeing him.*

PUCK *(stands up on stage left bench)*
Captain of our fairy band,
Helena is here at hand;
And the youth, mistook by me,
Pleading for a lover's fee.
Shall we their fond pageant see?
Lord, what fools these mortals be!

PUCK *jumps off bench. He and* **OBERON** *high five again, then hide behind stage right pillar.*

Enter **HELENA** *and* **LYSANDER** *from stage left. She sits with her back to him, facing stage right a little. He is to her left.*

LYSANDER
Why should you think that I should woo in scorn?

Scorn and derision never come in tears:
Look, when I vow, I weep.
> *(cries like a baby;* HELENA *turns around and looks at him with scorn and disbelief)*

HELENA *(stands)*
You do advance your cunning more and more.
When truth kills truth, O devilish-holy fray!
These vows are Hermia's: will you give her o'er?

LYSANDER
I had no judgment when to her I swore.
Demetrius loves her, and he loves not you.

DEMETRIUS *(awaking; he sees* HELENA *and comes at her lovingly)*
O Helen, goddess, nymph, perfect, divine!
Thy lips, those kissing cherries, tempting grow!
O, let me kiss
This princess of pure white, this seal of bliss!
> *(comes at her with puckered lips)*

HELENA *(stands stage center with both arms out trying to stiff-arm her suitors)*
O spite! O hell! I see you all are bent
To set against me for your merriment:
You both are rivals, and love Hermia;
And now both rivals, to mock Helena.
> *(lets go of the two men, who fall into each other, then push apart)*

LYSANDER
You are unkind, Demetrius; be not so;
For you love Hermia;- this you know I know:

DEMETRIUS
Lysander, keep thy Hermia; I will none:
If e'er I lov'd her, all that love is gone.

DEMETRIUS *(to* LYSANDER*)*
>Look, where thy love comes; yonder is thy dear.

Enter HERMIA *stage right.*

HERMIA
>Lysander, found;
>>*(she goes to* LYSANDER *with arms outstretched;*
>>LYSANDER *turns his back)*
>
>Mine ear, I thank it, brought me to thy sound.
>But why unkindly didst thou leave me so?

LYSANDER *(not turning)*
>Why should he stay, whom love doth press to go?

HERMIA *(grabs* LYSANDER'S *shoulder and turns him to face her)*
>What love could press Lysander from my side?

LYSANDER *turns* HERMIA *back around, she stumbles back and*
>*sits on bench.*
>
>Lysander's love, that would not let him bide,-
>>*(goes past Hermia to Helena)*
>
>Fair Helena; who more engilds the night
>Than all yon fiery O's and eyes of light.
>*(to Hermia)* Why seek'st thou me? could not this
>make thee know,
>The hate I bear thee made me leave thee so?

HERMIA *(can't believe this is happening)*
>You speak not as you think: it cannot be.

HELENA *(looks at* HERMIA *angrily, thinking she is mocking her)*
>Lo, she is one of this confederacy!
>Now I perceive they have conjoin'd all three
>To fashion this false sport in spite of me.
>>*(pushes the two men off her and starts*

toward HERMIA*)*
Injurious Hermia! most ungrateful maid!
Have you conspired, have you with these contrived
To bait me with this foul derision?

HERMIA *(taken aback and hurt)*
I am amazed at your passionate words.
I scorn you not: it seems that you scorn me.

HELENA
Have you not set Lysander, as in scorn,
To follow me, and praise my eyes and face?
And made your other love, Demetrius—
Who even but now did spurn me with his foot—
To call me goddess, nymph, divine, and rare.

LYSANDER
Stay, gentle Helena; hear my excuse:
My love, my life, my soul, fair Helena!

HELENA
O excellent!

HERMIA *(to* LYSANDER*)*
Sweet, do not scorn her so.

LYSANDER *(kneeling at* HELENA'S *feet)*
Helen, I love thee; by my life, I do.

DEMETRIUS *(also kneels at* HELENA'S *feet)*
I say I love thee more than he can do.

LYSANDER *(challenging him to a duel)*
If thou say so, withdraw, and prove it too.

They try to fight on their knees.

DEMETRIUS

Quick, come!

HERMIA

Lysander, whereto tends all this?
(she pulls LYSANDER *up to standing)*

LYSANDER *(to* HERMIA*)*

Hang off, thou cat, thou burr! vile thing, let loose,
Or I will shake thee from me like a serpent!

He tries to shake her loose, and she hangs onto his leg.

HERMIA

Am not I Hermia? are not you Lysander?
I am as fair now as I was erewhile.
Since night you loved me; yet since night you left me:

LYSANDER

Ay, by my life;
And never did desire to see thee more.
Be certain, nothing truer; 'tis no jest
That I do hate thee, and love Helena.

HERMIA *(to* HELENA*)*

O me!— you juggler! you canker-blossom!
You thief of love! what, have you come by night
And stol'n my love's heart from him?

HELENA *(standing over* HERMIA*)*

Fie, fie! you counterfeit, you puppet, you!

HERMIA

Puppet! why, so; ay, that way goes the game.
Now I perceive that she hath made compare
Between our statures; she hath urged her height;

And are you grown so high in his esteem,
Because I am so dwarfish and so low?
How low am I, thou painted maypole? Speak;
How low am I? I am not yet so low
But that my nails can reach unto thine eyes.

HERMIA *lunges at* HELENA, *fingernails out.*

HELENA *(hides behind the two men)*
I pray you, though you mock me, gentlemen,
Let her not hurt me:
You perhaps may think,
Because she is something lower than myself,
That I can match her.

HERMIA
Lower! hark, again.

HELENA
O, when she's angry, she is keen and shrewd!
And though she be but little, she is fierce.

HERMIA
Little again! Let me come to her.
            (comes at her again; the boys protect HELENA)

LYSANDER *(holding* HELENA *off)*
Get you gone, you dwarf;
You minimus, of hind'ring knot-grass made;
You bead, you acorn.

LYSANDER *(to* DEMETRIUS)
Now follow, if thou darest, to try whose right,
Of thine or mine, is most in Helena.

DEMETRIUS
Follow! nay, I'll go with thee, cheek by jowl.

Exeunt LYSANDER *and* DEMETRIUS, *pulling each other off stage rear.*

HELENA
Your hands than mine are quicker for a fray;
My legs are longer though, to run away.

Exit HELENA *stage left.*

HERMIA
I am amazed, and know not what to say.

Exit HERMIA *stage right.*

OBERON
This is thy negligence.

PUCK
Believe me, king of shadows, I mistook.

OBERON
Thou see'st these lovers seek a place to fight:
Hie therefore, Robin, overcast the night;
Then crush this herb into Lysander's eye;
And make his eyeballs roll with wonted sight.
When they next wake, all this derision
Shall seem a dream and fruitless vision.

Exit OBERON *stage rear.*

PUCK *(hopping up and down on benches)*
Up and down, up and down,
I will lead them up and down:
Here comes one.

Enter LYSANDER *stage right, ready to fight.*

LYSANDER
> Where art thou, proud Demetrius? speak thou now.

PUCK *(imitating* DEMETRIUS*)*
> Here, villain; drawn and ready.
> Follow me, then,
> To plainer ground.

PUCK *magically leads* LYSANDER *around in a circle until he gets dizzy and tired.*

LYSANDER
> When I come where he calls,
> then he is gone. *(yawns)* Here will I rest me.
> *(lies down and sleeps in front of stage right bench)*

Enter DEMETRIUS *stage left.*

DEMETRIUS (not seeing LYSANDER)
> Lysander! speak again:
> Thou runaway, thou coward, art thou fled?

PUCK

> Ho, ho, ho! Coward, why comest thou not?
> *(magically leading* DEMETRIUS *around until he gets dizzy, confused, and tired)*

DEMETRIUS
> Thou runn'st before me, shifting every place.
> Faintness constraineth me
> To measure out my length on this cold bed.
> *(lies down and sleeps in front of stage left bench)*

Enter HELENA *stage rear.*

HELENA

> O weary night, O long and tedious night,
> Sleep, that sometime shuts up sorrow's eye,
> Steal me awhile from mine own company.
>> *(lies down and sleeps downstage left in front of bench)*

PUCK

> Yet but three? Come one more;
> Two of both kinds makes up four.
> Here she comes, curst and sad:-
> Cupid is a knavish lad,
> Thus to make poor females mad.

Enter HERMIA *stage rear.*

HERMIA

> Never so weary, never so in woe;
> I can no further crawl, no further go;
> Here will I rest me till the break of day.
>> *(lies down and sleeps downstage right in front of bench)*

PUCK

> On the ground
> Sleep sound:
> I'll apply
> To your eye,
> Gentle lover, remedy.
>> *(squeezing the herb on* LYSANDER'S *eyelids)*

SOUND OPERATOR *plays* Sound Cue #3 (*"rrring" sound with chimes*).

> When thou wakest,
> Thou takest

True delight
In the sight
Of thy former lady's eye:

Exit PUCK *rear.*

✳ SCENE 2 (ACT IV, SCENE I)

Enter NARRATOR 2 *from rear and walk downstage center.*

NARRATOR 2
> Through magical fairie mischief, Bottom the Weaver
> has been transformed into an ass, and Titania,
> Queen of the fairies has fallen in love with him. We
> are still in the woods . . .

The wood. LYSANDER, DEMETRIUS, HELENA, *and* HERMIA, *lying
asleep. Enter* TITANIA *and* BOTTOM; PEAS-BLOSSOM, COBWEB,
MOTH, MUSTARD-SEED, *and other* FAIRIES *attending;* OBERON
behind unseen. All enter from stage rear.

TITANIA *(to* BOTTOM*)*
> Come, sit thee down upon this flowery bed,
> While I thy amiable cheeks do coy,
> And stick musk-roses in thy sleek smooth head,
> And kiss thy fair large ears, my gentle joy.

BOTTOM *lies on stage right bench, on his back, with face slightly
out to audience.*

TITANIA *sits on the bench up by* BOTTOM'S *head; she places a
flower behind his ear and kisses his big donkey ear.*

BOTTOM
> Where's Peas-blossom?

PEAS-BLOSSOM
> Ready.

BOTTOM

Scratch my head, Peas-blossom.
(she scratches his ears; he sighs, groans, and heehaws with pleasure)
Where's Monsieur Cobweb?

COBWEB

Ready.

BOTTOM

Monsieur Cobweb, good monsieur, get your
weapons in your hand, and kill me a red-hipp'd
humble-bee on the top of a thistle; and, good
monsieur, bring me the honey-bag.
Exit COBWEB *stage right.*
Where's Monsieur Mustard-Seed?

MUSTARD-SEED

What's your will?

BOTTOM

Nothing, good monsieur, but to help Cavalery Peas-
blossom to scratch.
*(*MUSTARDSEED *scratches* BOTTOM'S *ear; he sighs,
groans, and heehaws with pleasure)*
I must to the barber's, monsieur; for methinks I am
marvelous hairy about the face; and I am such a
tender ass, if my hair do but tickle me, I must scratch.

TITANIA

What, wilt thou hear some music, my sweet love?

BOTTOM

I have a reasonable good ear in music: let's have the
tongs and bones.

SOUND OPERATOR *plays* Sound Cue #4 *(New Age music).*

> *Fairies enter from rear, dance about* BOTTOM
> *with scarves and wands, and exit stage rear.*
> (BOTTOM *yawns)* I have an exposition of sleep come
> upon me.

TITANIA
> Sleep thou, and I will wind thee in my arms.-
> Fairies, be gone, and be all ways away.
> > *Exeunt* FAIRIES.
> O, how I love thee! how I dote on thee! *(they sleep)*

Enter PUCK *from rear, approaching* OBERON *on his right hand side.*

OBERON *(advancing toward sleeping* TITANIA *and* BOTTOM*)*
> Welcome, good Robin. See'st thou this sweet sight?
> Her dotage now I do begin to pity: I will undo
> This hateful imperfection of her eyes:
> And, gentle Puck, take this transformed scalp
> From off the head of this Athenian swain;
> That he, awaking when the other do,
> May all to Athens back again repair,
> And think no more of this night's accidents,
> But as the fierce vexation of a dream.
> But first I will release the fairy queen.
> Be as thou wast wont to be;
> > *(touching her eyes with an herb)*

SOUND OPERATOR *plays* Sound Cue # 5 *("shhhwwing" sound
with chimes).*

> See as thou wast wont to see:
> Now, my Titania: wake you, my sweet queen.

TITANIA *(awakening, groggy, and seeing* OBERON*)*
> My Oberon! what visions have I seen!
> Methought I was enamour'd of an ass.

OBERON *(pointing to* BOTTOM*)*
> There lies your love.

TITANIA *(shrieking and jumping up)*
> How came these things to pass?
> > *(she runs to stage left bench away from* BOTTOM*)*
> O, how mine eyes do loathe his visage now!
> > *(turns away, shields her eyes)*

OBERON
> Silence awhile.—Robin, take off this head.—
> Titania, music call; and strike more dead
> Than common sleep of all these five the sense.

TITANIA
> Music, ho! music, such as charmeth sleep.

SOUND OPERATOR *plays* Sound Cue #6 *(New Age Music).*

PUCK
> Now, when thou wakest, with thine own fool's eyes peep.
> > *(removes ass head from* BOTTOM, *who falls*
> > *back asleep)*

TITANIA
> Come, my lord; and in our flight,
> Tell me how it came this night
> That I sleeping here was found
> With these mortals on the ground.

Exit PUCK *and* TITANIA *stage right, holding hands.*

Enter THESEUS, HIPPOLYTA, EGEUS, *and* ATTENDANT *from rear.*

THESEUS

> We will, fair queen, up to the mountain's top,
> But, soft! what nymphs are these?
> > *(sees the two couples)*

EGEUS

> My lord, this is my daughter here asleep
> And this, Lysander; this Demetrius is;
> This Helena, I wonder of their being here together.

THESEUS *(to* ATTENDANT*)*
> Wake them.

ATTENDANT *shakes tambourine in couples' ears, and they wake, startled.*

LYSANDER

> Pardon, my lord.
> > *(sitting up, sees* THESEUS *and bows clumsily from a sitting position)*

THESEUS

> I pray you all, stand up.
> > *The two couples stand up, a little confused, and nervous.*
> I know you two are rival enemies:
> > LYSANDER *and* DEMETRIUS *look at each other as if to say, "What's up?", smile, and non-verbally congratulate each other on the other's woman.*
> How comes this gentle concord in the world,
> That hatred is so far from jealousy,
> To sleep by hate, and fear no enmity?

LYSANDER
> My lord,
> I cannot truly say how I came here;
> I came with Hermia hither
>> *(looks at* HERMIA *utterly googly-eyed)*

EGEUS *(angrily, almost shouting)*
> I beg the law, the law, upon his head.

DEMETRIUS
> But, my good lord, I wot not by what power,—
> But by some power it is,—my love to Hermia,
> Melted as the snow,
> And all the faith, the virtue of my heart,
> The object, and the pleasure of mine eye,
> Is only Helena.
>> *(looks at* HELENA *utterly googly-eyed)*

THESEUS
> Fair lovers, you are fortunately met:
> Egeus, I will overbear your will;
> For in the temple, by and by, with us
> These couples shall eternally be knit:
> Away with us to Athens! three and three,
> We'll hold a feast in great solemnity.
> Come, Hippolyta.

Exeunt THESEUS, HIPPOLYTA, EGEUS, *and* ATTENDANT *stage left.*

DEMETRIUS *(to* HELENA*)*
> Are you sure
> That we are awake? It seems to me
> That yet we sleep, we dream.-
> Let's follow him;
> And, by the way, let us recount our dreams.

Exeunt DEMETRIUS *and* HELENA *stage left.*

BOTTOM *(awaking)*

> I have had a most rare vision. I have had a dream,—
> past the wit of man to say what dream it was: man
> is but an ass, if he go about to expound this dream.
> Methought I was *(feels his face)* and methought I
> had *(feels his ears)* but man is but a patch'd fool, if
> he will offer to say what methought I had. I will
> get Peter Quince to write a ballad of this dream: it
> shall be called Bottom's Dream, because it hath no
> bottom; and I will sing it in the latter end of a play
> before the duke:

Exit BOTTOM *stage right.*

✳ SCENE 3 (ACT V, SCENE I)

STAGEHANDS ONE AND TWO *angle downstage right bench slightly sideways toward stage left.* STAGEHANDS THREE AND FOUR *remove bench from downstage.*

Enter NARRATOR 3 *from rear, coming downstage center.*

NARRATOR 3
> To complete our festive comedy, Bottom and the "rude mechanicals" perform the merry and tragical play of *Pyramus and Thisbe* for Theseus and Hippolyta and our newly married lovers. The fairies bless the three marriages and all is well. But still we wonder, has this all been a dream?

Athens. An apartment in the palace of Theseus. Enter THESEUS, HIPPOLYTA, PHILOSTRATE, LORDS, *and* ATTENDANTS *from stage rear. They settle in chairs stage right, with* THESEUS *to the right and* HIPPOLYTA *to the left.* EGEUS *sits in chair slightly behind and to the right.*

THESEUS
> Here come the lovers, full of joy and mirth.
> > *Enter* LYSANDER, DEMETRIUS, HERMIA, *and* HELENA. *They sit on the floor, with* LYSANDER *and* HERMIA *to the right and* DEMETRIUS *and* HELENA *to the left of the royal couple.*
> Come now; what masks, what dances shall we have,
> What revels are in hand? Call Philostrate.

PHILOSTRATE *(from stage right)*
> Here, mighty Theseus.

THESEUS
> Say, what abridgement have you for this evening?
> What mask? what music?

PHILOSTRATE
> Make choice of which your highness will see first.
> *(giving a paper)*

THESEUS *(reading)*
> "The battle with the Centaurs, to be sung
> By an Athenian eunuch to the harp."
> We'll none of that:
> *(reading)* "The riot of the tipsy Bacchanals,"
> That is an old device;
> *(reading)* "A tedious brief scene of young Pyramus
> And his love Thisbe; very tragical mirth."
> Merry and tragical! tedious and brief!
> That is, hot ice and wondrous strange snow.
> How shall we find the concord of this discord?

PHILOSTRATE
> A play there is, my lord, some ten words long,
> But by ten words, my lord, it is too long,
> There is not one word apt, one player fitted:

THESEUS
> What are they that do play it?

PHILOSTRATE
> Hard-handed men, that work in Athens here,
> Which never labour'd in their minds till now;

THESEUS
>And we will hear it.

PHILOSTRATE
>No, my noble lord;
>It is not for you: I have heard it over,
>And it is nothing, nothing in the world;

THESEUS
>I will hear that play;
>For never any thing can be amiss,
>When simpleness and duty tender it.
>Go, bring them in:-and take your places, ladies.

Exit PHILOSTRATE *stage rear.*

Great cheers emerge from backstage rear as MECHANICALS *discover their play has been chosen.*

Enter PHILOSTRATE *from rear.*

PHILOSTRATE
>So please your grace, the Prologue is address'd.

THESEUS
>Let him approach.

Enter the PROLOGUE *from rear.*

PROLOGUE
>If we offend, it is with our good will.
>That is the true beginning of our end.
>The actors are at hand; and, by their show,
>You shall know all that you are like to know.
>>*(stands uncomfortably, then slowly steps stage left)*

THESEUS
> This fellow doth not stand upon points.

LYSANDER
> He hath rid his prologue like a rough colt;

HIPPOLYTA
> Indeed he hath play'd on his prologue like a child
> on a recorder.

THESEUS
> Who is next?

Enter PYRAMUS *and* THISBE, WALL, MOONSHINE, *and* LION *from
rear. They stand stage left, nervously, a little behind pillar, except*
THISBE *who goes out stage right door.*

PROLOGUE
> Gentles, perchance you wonder at this show;
> But wonder on, till truth make all things plain.

WALL *(coming center)*
> In this same interlude it doth befall
> That I, one Snout by name, present a wall;
> And such a wall, as I would have you think,
> That had in it a crannied hole or chink,
> Through which the lovers, Pyramus and Thisbe,
> Did whisper often very secretly.

THESEUS
> Pyramus draws near the wall: silence!

Enter PYRAMUS *from left.*

PYRAMUS
> O grim-look'd night! O night with hue so black!

O night, which ever art when day is not!
I fear my Thisbe's promise is forgot!—
And thou, O wall, O sweet, O lovely wall,
That stand'st between her father's ground and mine!
Show me thy chink, to blink through with mine eyne!
    WALL *holds up his fingers.*
Thanks, courteous wall: Jove shield thee well for this!
But what see I? No Thisbe do I see.
O wicked wall, through whom I see no bliss!
    He whacks WALL. WALL *smacks him back.*
Cursed be thy stones for thus deceiving me!

Enter THISBE.

THISBE

O wall, full often hast thou heard my moans,
My cherry lips have often kiss'd thy stones.

He kisses WALL. WALL *giggles and blushes.*

PYRAMUS

I see a voice: now will I to the chink,
To spy an I can hear my Thisbe's face.—
Thisbe!

THISBE

My love! thou art my love, I think.

PYRAMUS

O, kiss me through the hole of this vile wall!

THISBE

I kiss the wall's hole, not your lips at all.

THISBE *and* PYRAMUS *both kiss* WALL'S *hand, exclaiming "Ptooee!" and grimacing.* WALL, *confused, smells his own hand and looks a little hurt.*

PYRAMUS
Wilt thou at Ninny's tomb meet me straightway?

QUINCE *(exasperated, walking onto the stage, correcting him)*
Ninus' Tomb!

THISBE
'Tide life, 'tide death, I come without delay.

Exeunt PYRAMUS *stage left and* THISBE *stage right.*

WALL
Thus have I, wall, my part discharged so;
And, being done, thus wall away doth go.

Exit WALL *stage left, getting stuck in doorway.*

HIPPOLYTA
This is the silliest stuff that e'er I heard.

THESEUS
Here come two noble beasts in, a moon and a lion.

Enter LION *and* MOONSHINE *from stage left pillar.*

LION
You, ladies may now perchance both quake
and tremble here,
When lion rough in wildest rage doth roar.
(aside to royal crew) Then know that I one
Snug the joiner am,

THESEUS
> A very gentle beast, and of a good conscience.
> Let us listen to the moon.

MOONSHINE *(angrily)*
> This lantern doth the horned moon present;
> Myself the man-i'-th'-moon do seem to be.

HIPPOLYTA *(interrupting; to* **THESEUS***, but* **MOON** *can hear her)*
> I am aweary of this moon. Would he would change.

LYSANDER
> Proceed, moon.

MOONSHINE
> All that I have to say is, to tell you that the lantern
> is the moon; I, the man-i'-th'-moon; this thorn-bush,
> my thorn-bush; and this dog, my dog.

DEMETRIUS
> Here comes Thisbe.

Enter **THISBE** *from stage right.*

THISBE
> This is old Ninny's tomb.

QUINCE *(more exasperated, returning to stage)*
> Ninus' tomb, man!

THISBE
> This is old Ninnies' tomb!. Where is my love?

QUINCE *cries out, "Aarrrgh!" from backstage.*

LION
>   O—

LION *roars and* THISBE *runs off.*

A chaotic chase scene spills into audience. LION *chases* THISBE, *then chases* PHILOSTRATE. *There is a great commotion in Royal audience.* MOON *runs behind them, trying to light their way.*

DEMETRIUS
>   Well roar'd, lion.

THESEUS
>   Well run, Thisbe.

HIPPOLYTA
>   Well shone, moon.

LION *tears* THISBE'S *mantle and exits stage rear.*

THESEUS
>   Well moused, lion.

DEMETRIUS
>   And then came Pyramus.

Enter PYRAMUS *from stage left pillar.*

PYRAMUS
>   Sweet moon, I thank thee for thy sunny beams;
>   But mark, poor knight,
>   What dreadful dole is here!
>   Eyes, do you see?
>   How can it be?
>   O dainty duck! O dear!
>   Thy mantle good,

What, stain'd with blood?
Come, tears, confound;
Out, sword, and wound
The pap of Pyramus,—
Ay, that left pap,
Where heart doth hop: *(stabs himself)*
Thus die I, thus, thus.

> *Long pause. Audience is about to clap when*
> **PYRAMUS** *springs back up. Audience gasps*
> *and shrieks.*

Now am I dead,
Now am I fled;
My soul is in the sky:
Tongue, lose thy light;
Moon, take thy flight:

> *Exit* **MOONSHINE.**

Now die, die, die, die, die. *(dies)*

THESEUS

With the help of a surgeon he might yet recover,
and yet prove an ass.

THISBE *(entering from left)*

Asleep, my love?
What, dead my dove?
O Pyramus, arise!
Speak, speak. Quite dumb?
Dead, dead? A tomb
Must cover thy sweet eyes.
His eyes were green as leeks.
Come, trusty sword;
Come, blade, my breast imbrue *(stabs herself)*
And, farewell, friends,—
Thus Thisbe ends,-
Adieu, adieu, adieu. *(dies)*

BOTTOM *(gets up with the sword still in him; to* **THESEUS***)*
> Will it please you to see the epilogue, or to hear a
> Bergomask dance between two of our company?

THESEUS
> No epilogue, I pray you; for your play needs no excuse.

SOUND OPERATOR *plays* Sound Cue #7 *(a bell ringing twelve times).*

> The iron tongue of midnight hath told twelve:
> Lovers, to bed; 'tis almost fairy-time.

All freeze as fairies enter. Enter **PUCK**, **OBERON**, *and* **TITANIA**, *with their* **TRAIN**, *from stage rear.*

OBERON
> Now, until the break of day,
> Through this house each fairy stray.
> So shall all the couples three
> Ever true in loving be;
> > **PUCK** *magically waves hand*

SOUND OPERATOR *plays* Sound Cue #8 *("brrring" effect).*

> > *and* **LOVERS** *move closer and hold hands.* **PUCK**
> > *waves his hands again and the music starts up.*
> > *All awake and begin to move in rhythm.*
> If we shadows have offended,
> Think but this, and all is mended,-
> That you have but slumber'd here,
> While these visions did appear.
> And this weak and idle theme,
> No more yielding but a dream,
> So, good night unto you all.
> Give me your hands, if we be friends,

PUCK
And Robin shall restore amends!

ALL REPEAT (holding hands and raising them joyously)
And Robin shall restore amends!

Great rejoicing and merriment!

All raise arms holding hands, and bow.

✳ PERFORMING SHAKESPEARE

BACKGROUND:
HOW *THE 30-MINUTE SHAKESPEARE* WAS BORN

In 1981 I performed a "Shakespeare Juggling" piece called "To Juggle or Not To Juggle" at the first Folger Library Secondary School Shakespeare Festival. The audience consisted of about 200 Washington, D.C. area high school students who had just performed thirty-minute versions of Shakespeare plays for each other and were jubilant over the experience. I was dressed in a jester's outfit, and my job was to entertain them. I juggled and jested and played with Shakespeare's words, notably Hamlet's "To be or not to be" soliloquy, to very enthusiastic response. I was struck by how much my "Shakespeare Juggling" resonated with a group who had just performed Shakespeare themselves. "Getting" Shakespeare is a heady feeling, especially for adolescents, and I am continually delighted at how much joy and satisfaction young people derive from performing Shakespeare. Simply reading and studying this great playwright does not even come close to inspiring the kind of enthusiasm that comes from performance.

Surprisingly, many of these students were not "actor types." A good percentage of the students performing Shakespeare that day were part of an English class which had rehearsed the plays during class time. Fifteen years later, when I first started directing plays in D.C. public schools as a Teaching Artist with the Folger Shakespeare Library, I entered a ninth grade English class as a guest and spent two or three days a week for two or three months preparing students for the Folger's annual Secondary School Shakespeare Festival. I have conducted this annual residency with the Folger ever since.

Every year for seven action-packed days, eight groups of students between grades seven and twelve tread the boards onstage at the Folger's Elizabethan Theatre, a grand recreation of a sixteenth-century venue with a three-tiered gallery, carved oak columns, and a sky-painted canopy.

As noted on the Folger website (www.folger.edu), "The festival is a celebration of the Bard, not a competition. Festival commentators—drawn from the professional theater and Shakespeare education communities—recognize exceptional performances, student directors, and good spirit amongst the students with selected awards at the end of each day. They are also available to share feedback with the students."

My annual Folger Teaching Artist engagement, directing a Shakespeare play in a public high school English class, is the most challenging and the most rewarding thing I do all year. I hope this book can bring you the same rewards.

GETTING STARTED: GAMES

How can you get an English class (or any other group of young people, or even adults) to start the seemingly daunting task of performing a Shakespeare play? You have already successfully completed the critical first step, which is buying this book. You hold in your hand a performance-ready, thirty-minute cutting of a Shakespeare play, with stage directions to get the actors moving about the stage purposefully. But it's a good idea to warm the group up with some theater games.

One good initial exercise is called "Positive/Negative Salutations." Students stand in two lines facing each other (four or five students in each line) and, reading from index cards, greet each other, first with a "Positive" salutation in Shakespeare's language (using actual phrases from the plays), followed by a "negative" greeting.

Additionally, short vocal exercises are an essential part of the preparation process. The following is a very simple and effective vocal warm-up: Beginning with the number two, have the whole group count to twenty using increments of two (i.e., "Two, four, six . . ."). Increase the volume slightly with each number, reaching top volume with "twenty," and then decrease the volume while counting back down, so that the students are practically whispering when they arrive again at "two." This exercise teaches dynamics and allows them to get loud as a group without any individual pressure. Frequently during a rehearsal period, if a student is mumbling inaudibly, I will refer back to this exercise as a reminder that we can and often do belt it out!

"Stomping Words" is a game that is very helpful at getting a handle on Shakespeare's rhythm. Choose a passage in iambic pentameter and have the group members walk around the room in a circle, stomping their feet on the second beat of each line:

Two **house**-holds, **both** a-**like** in **dig**-nity
In **fair** Ve-**ro**na **Where** we **lay** our **scene**

Do the same thing with a prose passage, and have the students discuss their experience with it, including points at which there is an extra beat, etc., and what, if anything, it might signify.

I end every vocal warm-up with a group reading of one of the speeches from the play, emphasizing diction and projection, bouncing off consonants, and encouraging the group members to listen to each other so that they can speak the lines together in unison. For variety I will throw in some classic "tongue twisters" too, such as, "The sixth sheik's sixth sheep is sick."

The Folger Shakespeare Library's website (http://www.folger.edu) and their book series *Shakespeare Set Free,* edited by Peggy O'Brien, are two great resources for getting started with a performance-based teaching of Shakespeare in the classroom. The Folger website has numerous helpful resources and activities, many submitted by teachers, for helping a class actively participate in the process of getting to know a Shakespeare play. For more simple theater games, Viola Spolin's *Theatre Games for the Classroom* is very helpful, as is one I use frequently, *Theatre Games for Young Performers*.

HATS AND PROPS

Introducing a few hats and props early in the process is a good way to get the action going. Hats, in particular, provide a nice avenue for giving young actors a non-verbal way of getting into character. In the opening weeks, when students are still holding onto their scripts, a hat can give an actor a way to "feel" like a character. Young actors are natural masters at injecting their own personality into what they wear, and even small choices made with how a hat is worn (jauntily, shadily, cockily, mysteriously) provide a starting point for discussion of specific characters, their traits, and their relationships with other characters. All such discussions always lead back to one thing: the text. "Mining the text" is consistently the best strategy for uncovering the mystery of Shakespeare's language. That is where all the answers lie: in the words themselves.

WHAT DO THE WORDS MEAN?

It is essential that young actors know what they are saying when they recite Shakespeare. If not, they might as well be scat singing, riffing on sounds and rhythm but not conveying a specific meaning. The real question is: What do the words mean? The answer is multifaceted, and can be found in more than one place. The New Folger Library paperback editions of the plays themselves (edited by Barbara Mowat and Paul Werstine, Washington Square Press) are a great resource for understanding Shakespeare's words and passages and "translating" them into modern English. These editions also contain chapters on Shakespeare's language, his life, his theater, a "Modern Perspective," and further reading. There is a wealth of scholarship embedded in these wonderful books, and I make it a point to read them cover to cover before embarking on a play-directing project. At the very least, it is a good idea for any adult who intends to direct a Shakespeare play with a group of students to go through the explanatory notes that appear on the pages facing the text. These explanatory notes are an indispensable "translation tool."

The best way to get students to understand what Shakespeare's words mean is to ask them what they think they mean. Students have their own associations with the words and with how they sound and feel. The best ideas on how to perform Shakespeare often come directly from the students, not from anybody else's notion. If a student has an idea or feeling about a word or passage, and it resonates with her emotionally, physically, or spiritually, then Shakespeare's words can be a vehicle for her feelings. That can result in some powerful performances!

I make it my job as director to read the explanatory notes in the Folger text, but I make it clear to the students that almost "anything goes" when trying to understand Shakespeare. There are no wrong interpretations. Students have their own experiences, with some shared and some uniquely their own. If someone has an association with the phrase "canker-blossom," or if the words make that student or his character feel or act a certain way, then that is the "right" way to decipher it.

I encourage the students to refer to the Folger text's explanatory notes and to keep a pocket dictionary handy. Young actors must attach some meaning to every word or line they recite. If I feel an actor is glossing over a word, I will stop him and ask him what he is saying. If he doesn't know, we will figure it out together as a group.

PROCESS VS. PRODUCT

The process of learning Shakespeare by performing one of his plays is more important than whether everybody remembers his lines or whether somebody misses a cue or an entrance. But my Teaching Artist residencies have always had the end goal of a public performance for about 200 other students, so naturally the performance starts to take precedence over the process somewhere around Dress Rehearsal in the students' minds. It is my job to make sure the actors are prepared—otherwise they will remember the embarrassing moment of a public mistake and not the glorious triumph of owning a Shakespeare play.

In one of my earlier years of play directing, I was sitting in the audience as one of my narrators stood frozen on stage for at least a minute, trying to remember her opening line. I started scrambling in my backpack below my seat for a script, at last prompting her from the audience. Despite her fine performance, that embarrassing moment is all she remembered from the whole experience. Since then I have made sure to assign at least one person to prompt from backstage if necessary. Additionally, I inform the entire cast that if somebody is dying alone out there, it is okay to rescue him or her with an offstage prompt.

There is always a certain amount of stage fright that will accompany a performance, especially a public one for an unfamiliar audience. As a director, I live with stage fright as well, even though I am not appearing on stage. The only antidote to this is work and preparation. If a young actor is struggling with her lines, I make sure to arrange for a session where we run lines over the telephone. I try to set up a buddy system so that students can run lines with their peers, and this often works well. But if somebody does not have a "buddy," I will personally make the time to help out myself. As I assure my students from the outset, I am not going to let them fail or embarrass themselves. They need an experienced leader. And if the leader has experience in teaching but not in directing Shakespeare, then he needs this book!

It is a good idea to culminate in a public performance, as opposed to an in-class project, even if it is only for another classroom. Student actors want to show their newfound Shakespearian thespian skills to an outside group, and this goal motivates them to do a good job. In that respect, "product" is important. Another wonderful bonus to performing a play is that it is a unifying group effort. Students learn teamwork. They learn to give focus to another actor when he is speaking, and to play off of other characters. I like to end each performance with the entire cast reciting a passage in unison. This is a powerful ending, one that reaffirms the unity of the group.

SEEING SHAKESPEARE PERFORMED

It is very helpful for young actors to see Shakespeare performed by a group of professionals, whether they are appearing live on stage (preferable but not always possible) or on film. Because an entire play can take up two or more full class periods, time may be an issue. I am fortunate because thanks to a local foundation that underwrites theater education in the schools, I have been able to take my school groups to a Folger Theatre matinee of the play that they are performing. I always pick a play that is being performed locally that season. But not all group leaders are that lucky. Fortunately, there is the Internet, specifically YouTube. A quick YouTube search for "Shakespeare" can unearth thousands of results, many appropriate for the classroom.

The first "Hamlet" result showed an 18-year-old African-American actor on the streets of Camden, New Jersey, delivering a riveting performance of Hamlet's "The play's the thing." The second clip was from *Cat Head Theatre,* an animation of cats performing Hamlet. Of course, YouTube boasts not just alley cats and feline thespians, but also clips by true legends of the stage, such as John Gielgud and Richard Burton. These clips can be saved and shown in classrooms, providing useful inspiration.

One advantage of the amazing variety of clips available on YouTube is that students can witness the wide range of interpretations for any given scene, speech, or character in Shakespeare, thus freeing them from any preconceived notion that there is a "right" way to do it.

Furthermore, modern interpretations of the Bard may appeal to those who are put off by the "thees and thous" of Elizabethan speech.

By seeing Shakespeare performed either live or on film, students are able to hear the cadence, rhythm, vocal dynamics, and pronunciation of the language, and they can appreciate the life that other actors breathe into the characters. They get to see the story told dramatically, which inspires them to tell their own version.

PUTTING IT ALL TOGETHER: THE STEPS

After a few sessions of theater games to warm up the group, it's time to begin the process of casting the play. Each play cutting in *The 30-Minute Shakespeare* series includes a cast list and a sample program, demonstrating which parts have been divided. Cast size is generally between twenty and thirty students, with major roles frequently assigned to more than one performer. In other words, one student may play Juliet in the first scene, another in the second scene, and yet another in the third. This will distribute the parts evenly so that there is no "star of the show." Furthermore, this prevents actors from being burdened with too many lines. If I have an actor who is particularly talented or enthusiastic, I will give her a bigger role. It is important to go with the grain—one cast member's enthusiasm can be contagious.

I provide the performer of each shared role with a similar headpiece and/or cape, so that the audience can keep track of the characters. When there are sets of twins, I try to use blue shirts and red shirts, so that the audience has at least a fighting chance of figuring it out! Other than these costume consistencies, I rely on the text and the audience's observance to sort out the doubling of characters. Generally, the audience can follow because we are telling the story.

Some participants are shy and do not wish to speak at all on stage. To these students I assign non-speaking parts and technical roles such as sound operator and stage manager. However, I always get everybody on stage at some point, even if it is just for the final group speech, because I want every group member to experience what it is like to be on a stage as part of an ensemble.

CASTING THE PLAY

Young people can be self-conscious and nervous with "formal" auditions, especially if they have little or no acting experience.

I conduct what I call an "informal" audition process. I hand out a questionnaire asking students if there is any particular role that they desire, whether they play a musical instrument. To get a feel for them as people, I also ask them to list one or two hobbies or interests. Occasionally this will inform my casting decisions. If someone can juggle, and the play has the part of a Fool, that skill may come in handy. Dancing or martial arts abilities can also be applied to roles.

For the auditions, I do not use the cut script. I have students stand and read from the Folger edition of the complete text in order to hear how they fare with the longer passages. I encourage them to breathe and carry their vocal energy all the way to the end of a long line of text. I also urge them to play with diction, projection, modulation, and dynamics, elements of speech that we have worked on in our vocal warm-ups and theater games.

I base my casting choices largely on reading ability, vocal strength, and enthusiasm for the project. If someone has requested a particular role, I try to honor that request. I explain that even with a small part, an actor can create a vivid character that adds a lot to the play. Wide variations in personality types can be utilized: if there are two students cast as Romeo, one brooding and one effusive, I try to put the more brooding Romeo in an early lovelorn scene, and place the effusive Romeo in the balcony scene. Occasionally one gets lucky, and the doubling of characters provides a way to match personality types with different aspects of a character's personality. But also be aware of the potential serendipity of non-traditional casting. For example,

I have had one of the smallest students in the class play a powerful Othello. True power comes from within!

Generally, I have more females than males in a class, so women are more likely (and more willing) to play male characters than vice versa. Rare is the high school boy who is brave enough to play a female character, which is unfortunate because it can reap hilarious results.

GET OUTSIDE HELP

Every time there is a fight scene in one of the plays I am directing, I call on my friend Michael Tolaydo, a professional actor and theater professor at St. Mary's College, who is an expert in all aspects of theater, including fight choreography. Not only does Michael stage the fight, but he does so in a way that furthers the action of the play, highlighting character's traits and bringing out the best in the student actors. Fight choreography must be done by an expert or somebody could get hurt. In the absence of such help, super slow-motion fights are always a safe bet and can be quite effective, especially when accompanied by a soundtrack on the boom box.

During dress rehearsals I invite my friend Hilary Kacser. a Washington-area actor and dialect coach for two decades. Because I bring her in late in the rehearsal process, I have her direct her comments to me, which I then filter and relay to the cast. This avoids confusing the cast with a second set of directions. This caveat only applies to general directorial comments from outside visitors. Comments on specific artistic disciplines such as dance, music, and stage combat can come from the outside experts themselves.

If you work in a school, you might have helpful resources within your own building, such as a music or dance teacher who could contribute their expertise to a scene. If nobody is available in your school, try seeking out a member of the local professional theater. Many local performing artists will be glad to help, and the students are usually thrilled to have a visit from a professional performer.

LET STUDENTS BRING THEMSELVES INTO THE PLAY

The best ideas often come from the students themselves. If a young actor has a notion of how to play a scene, I will always give that idea a try. In a rehearsal of *Henry IV, Part 1,* one traveler jumped into the other's arms when they were robbed. It got a huge laugh. This was something that they did on instinct. We kept that bit for the performance, and it worked wonderfully.

As a director, you have to foster an environment in which that kind of spontaneity can occur. The students have to feel safe to experiment. In the same production of *Henry IV,* Falstaff and Hal invented a little fist bump "secret handshake" to use in the battle scene. The students were having fun and bringing parts of themselves into the play. Shakespeare himself would have approved. When possible I try to err on the side of fun because if the young actors are having fun, then they will commit themselves to the project. The beauty of the language, the story, the characters, and the pathos will follow.

There is a balance to be achieved here, however. In that same production of *Henry IV, Part 1,* the student who played Bardolph was having a great time with her character. She carried a leather wineskin around and offered it up to the other characters in the tavern. It was a prop with which she developed a comic relationship. At the end of our thirty-minute *Henry IV, Part 1,* I added a scene from *Henry IV, Part 2* as a coda: The new King Henry V (formerly Falstaff's drinking and carousing buddy Hal) rejects Falstaff, banishing him from within ten miles of the King. It is a sad and sobering moment, one of the most powerful in the play.

But at the performance, in the middle of the King's rejection speech (played by a female student, and her only speech), Bardolph offered her flask to King Henry and got a big laugh, thus not only upstaging the King but also undermining the seriousness and poignancy of the whole scene. She did not know any better; she was bringing herself to the character as I had been encouraging her to do. But it was inappropriate, and in subsequent seasons, if I foresaw something like that happening as an individual joyfully occupied a character, I attempted to prevent it. Some things we cannot predict. Now I make sure to issue a statement warning against changing any of the blocking on show day, and to watch out for upstaging one's peers.

FOUR FORMS OF ENGAGEMENT: VOCAL, EMOTIONAL, PHYSICAL, AND INTELLECTUAL

When directing a Shakespeare play with a group of students, I always start with the words themselves because the words have the power to engage the emotions, mind, and body. Also, I start with the words in action, as in the previously mentioned exercise, "Positive and Negative Salutations." Students become physically engaged; their bodies react to the images the words evoke. The words have the power to trigger a switch in both the teller and the listener, eliciting both an emotional and physical reaction. I have never heard a student utter the line "Fie! Fie! You counterfeit, you puppet you!" without seeing him change before my eyes. His spine stiffens, his eyes widen, and his fingers point menacingly.

Having used Shakespeare's words to engage the students emotionally and physically, one can then return to the text for a more reflective discussion of what the words mean to us personally. I always make sure to leave at least a few class periods open for discussion of the text, line by line, to ensure that students understand intellectually what they feel viscerally. The advantage to a performance-based teaching of Shakespeare is that by engaging students vocally, emotionally, and physically, it is then much easier to engage them intellectually because they are invested in the words, the characters, and the story. We always start on our feet, and later we sit and talk.

SIX ELEMENTS OF DRAMA: PLOT, CHARACTER, THEME, DICTION, MUSIC, AND SPECTACLE

Over two thousand years ago, Aristotle's *Poetics* outlined six elements of drama, in order of importance: Plot, Character, Theme, Diction, Music, and Spectacle. Because Shakespeare was foremost a playwright, it is helpful to take a brief look at these six elements as they relate to directing a Shakespeare play in the classroom.

PLOT (ACTION)

To Aristotle, plot was the most important element. One of the purposes of *The 30-Minute Shakespeare* is to provide a script that tells Shakespeare's stories, as opposed to concentrating on one scene. In a thirty-minute edit of a Shakespeare play, some plot elements are necessarily omitted. For the sake of a full understanding of the characters' relationships and motivations, it is helpful to make short plot summaries of each scene so that students are aware of their characters' arcs throughout the play. The scene descriptions in the Folger editions are sufficient to fill in the plot holes. Students can read the descriptions aloud during class time to ensure that the story is clear and that no plot elements are neglected. Additionally, there are one-page charts in the Folger editions of *Shakespeare Set Free*, indicating characters' relations graphically, with lines connecting families and factions to give students a visual representation of what can often be complex interrelationships, particularly in Shakespeare's history plays.

Young actors love action. That is why *The 30-Minute Shakespeare* includes dynamic blocking (stage direction) that allows students to tell the story in a physically dramatic fashion. Characters' movements on the stage are always motivated by the text itself.

CHARACTER

I consider myself a facilitator and a director more than an acting teacher. I want the students' understanding of their characters to spring from the text and the story. From there, I encourage them to consider how their character might talk, walk, stand, sit, eat, and drink. I also urge students to consider characters' motivations, objectives, and relationships, and I will ask pointed questions to that end during the rehearsal process. I try not to show the students how I would perform a scene, but if no ideas are forthcoming from anybody in the class, I will suggest a minimum of two possibilities for how the character might respond.

At times students may want more guidance and examples. Over thirteen years of directing plays in the classroom, I have wavered between wanting all the ideas to come from the students, and deciding that I need to be more of a "director," telling them what I would like to see them doing. It is a fine line, but in recent years I have decided that if I don't see enough dynamic action or characterization, I will step in and "direct" more. But I always make sure to leave room for students to bring themselves into the characters because their own ideas are invariably the best.

THEME (THOUGHTS, IDEAS)

In a typical English classroom, theme will be a big topic for discussion of a Shakespeare play. Using a performance-based method of teaching Shakespeare, an understanding of the play's themes develops from "mining the text" and exploring Shakespeare's words and his story. If the students understand what they are saying and how that relates to their characters and the overall story, the plays' themes will emerge clearly. We always return to the text itself. There are a number of elegant computer programs, such as www.wordle.net, that will count the number of recurring words in a passage and illustrate them graphically. For example, if the word "jealousy" comes up more than any other word in *Othello,* it will appear in a larger font. Seeing the words displayed by size in this way can offer up illuminating insights into the interaction between words in the text and the play's themes. Your computer-minded students might enjoy searching for such tidbits. There are more internet tools and websites in the Additional Resources section at the back of this book.

I cannot overstress the importance of acting out the play in understanding its themes. By embodying the roles of Othello and Iago and reciting their words, students do not simply comprehend the themes intellectually, but understand them kinesthetically, physically, and emotionally. They are essentially **living** the characters' jealousy, pride, and feelings about race. The themes of appearance vs. reality, good vs. evil, honesty, misrepresentation, and self-knowledge (or lack thereof) become physically felt as well as intellectually understood. Performing Shakespeare delivers a richer understanding than that which comes from just reading the play. Students can now relate the characters' conflicts to their own struggles.

DICTION (LANGUAGE)

If I had to cite one thing I would like my actors to take from their experience of performing a play by William Shakespeare, it is an appreciation and understanding of the beauty of Shakespeare's language. The language is where it all begins and ends. Shakespeare's stories are dramatic, his characters are rich and complex, and his settings are exotic and fascinating, but it is through his language that these all achieve their richness. This leads me to spend more time on language than on any other element of the performance.

Starting with daily vocal warm-ups, many of them using parts of the script or other Shakespearean passages, I consistently emphasize the importance of the words. Young actors often lack experience in speaking clearly and projecting their voices outward, so in addition to comprehension, I emphasize projection, diction, breathing, pacing, dynamics, coloring of words, and vocal energy. *Theatre Games for Young Performers* contains many effective vocal exercises, as does the Folger's *Shakespeare Set Free* series. Consistent emphasis on all aspects of Shakespeare's language, especially on how to speak it effectively, is the most important element to any Shakespeare performance with a young cast.

MUSIC

A little music can go a long way in setting a mood for a thirty-minute Shakespeare play. I usually open the show with a short passage of music to set the tone. Thirty seconds of music played on a boom box operated by a student can provide a nice introduction to the play, create an atmosphere for the audience, and give the actors a sense of place and feeling.

iTunes is a good starting point for choosing your music. Typing in "Shakespeare" or "Hamlet" or "jealousy" (if you are going for a theme) will result in an excellent selection of aural performance enhancers at the very reasonable price of ninety-nine cents each (or free of charge, see Additional Resources section.) Likewise, fight sounds, foreboding sounds, weather sounds (rain, thunder), trumpet sounds, etc. are all readily available online at affordable cost. I typically include three sound cues in a play, just enough to enhance but not overpower a production. The boom box operator sits on the far right or left of the stage, not backstage, so he can see the action. This also has the added benefit of having somebody out there with a script, capable of prompting in a pinch.

SPECTACLE

Aristotle considered spectacle the least important aspect of drama. Students tend to be surprised at this since we are used to being bombarded with production values on TV and video, often at the expense of substance. In my early days of putting on student productions, I would find myself hamstrung by my own ambitions in the realm of scenic design.

A simple bench or two chairs set on the stage are sufficient. The sense of "place" can be achieved through language and acting. Simple set dressing, a few key props, and some tasteful, emblematic costume pieces will go a long way toward providing all the "spectacle" you need.

In the stage directions to the plays in *The 30-Minute Shakespeare* series, I make frequent use of two large pillars stage left and right at the Folger Shakespeare Library's Elizabethan Theatre. I also have characters frequently entering and exiting from "stage rear." Your stage will have a different layout. Take a good look at the performing space you will be using and see if there are any elements that can be incorporated into your own stage directions. Is there a balcony? Can characters enter from the audience? (Make sure that they can get there from backstage, unless you want them waiting in the lobby until their entrance, which may be impractical.) If possible, make sure to rehearse in that space a few times to fix any technical issues and perhaps discover a few fun staging variations that will add pizzazz and dynamics to your own show.

The real spectacle is in the telling of the tale. Wooden swords are handy for characters that need them. Students should be warned at the outset that playing with swords outside of the scene is verboten. Letters, moneybags, and handkerchiefs should all have plentiful duplicates kept in a small prop box, as well as with a stage manager, because they tend to disappear in the hands of adolescents. After every rehearsal and performance, I recommend you personally sweep the rehearsal or performance area immediately for stray props. It is amazing what gets left behind.

Ultimately, the performances are about language and human drama, not set pieces, props, and special effects. Fake blood, glitter, glass, and liquids have no place on the stage; they are a recipe for disaster, or, at the very least, a big mess. On the other hand, the props that are employed can often be used effectively to convey character, as in Bardolph's aforementioned relationship with his wineskin.

PITFALLS AND SOLUTIONS

Putting on a play in a high school classroom is not easy. There are problems with enthusiasm, attitude, attention, and line memorization, to name a few. As anybody who has directed a play will tell you, it is always darkest before the dawn. My experience is that after one or two days of utter despair just before the play goes up, show day breaks and the play miraculously shines. To quote a recurring gag in one of my favorite movies, *Shakespeare in Love:* "It's a mystery."

ENTHUSIASM, FRUSTRATION, AND DISCIPLINE

Bring the enthusiasm yourself. Feed on the energy of the eager students, and others will pick up on that. Keep focused on the task at hand. Arrive prepared. Enthusiasm comes as you make headway. Ultimately, it helps to remind the students that a "play" is fun. I try to focus on the positive attributes of the students, rather than the ones that drive me crazy. This is easier said than done, but it is important. One season, I yelled at the group two days in a row. On day two of yelling, they tuned me out, and it took me a while to win them back. I learned my lesson; since then I've tried not to raise my voice out of anger or frustration. As I grow older and more mature, it is important for me to lead by example. It has been years since I yelled at a student group. If I am disappointed in their work or their behavior, I will express my disenchantment in words, speaking from the heart as somebody who cares about them and cares about our performance and our experience together. I find that fundamentally, young people want to please, to do well, and to be liked. If there is a serious discipline problem, I will hand it over to the regular classroom teacher, the administrator, or the parent.

LINE MEMORIZATION

Students may have a hard time memorizing lines. In these cases, see if you can pair them up with a "buddy" and existing friend who will run lines with them in person or over the phone after school. If students do not have such a "buddy," I volunteer to run lines with them myself. If serious line memorization problems arise that cannot be solved through work, then two students can switch parts if it is early enough in the rehearsal process. For doubled roles, the scene with fewer lines can go to the actor who is having memorization problems. Additionally, a few passages or lines can be cut. Again, it is important to address these issues early. Later cuts become more problematic as other actors have already memorized their cues. I have had to do late cuts about twice in thirteen years. While they have gotten us out of jams, it is best to assess early whether a student will have line memorization problems, and deal with the problem sooner rather than later.

In production, always keep several copies of the script backstage, as well as cheat sheets indicating cues, entrances, and scene changes. Make a prop list, indicating props for each scene, as well as props that are the responsibility of individual actors. Direct the Stage Manager and an Assistant Stage Manager to keep track of these items, and on show days, personally double-check if you can.

In thirteen years of preparing an inner-city public high school English class for a public performance on a field trip to the Folger Secondary School Shakespeare Festival, my groups and I have been beset by illness, emotional turmoil, discipline problems, stage fright, adolescent angst, midlife crises (not theirs), and all manner of other emergencies, including acts of God and nature. Despite the difficulties and challenges inherent in putting on a Shakespeare play with a group of young people, one amazing fact stands out in my experience. Here is how many times a student has been absent for show day: Zero. Somehow, everybody has always made it to the show, and the show has gone on. How can this be? It's a mystery.

✳ PERFORMANCE NOTES:
A MIDSUMMER NIGHT'S DREAM

I directed this thirty-minute production of *A Midsummer Night's Dream* in the year 2000 with a group of ninth graders. The play is colorful, fanciful, and magical, and students have a lot of fun bringing the fantasy to life. The first scene is actually several small scenes rolled into one, so it is important to keep the entrances and exits crisp. The stage should never be empty. I liken it to a relay race: the runner receiving the baton starts to run before he receives it. Likewise, as an actor or group of actors leaves the stage, the next group should be entering. Especially in a madcap story like this one, the pace should be quick and the energy high. It is a dream, after all, so everything that happens is beyond the realm of mortal understanding!

These notes are the result of my own review of the performance video. They are not intended to be the "definitive" performance notes for all productions of *A Midsummer Night's Dream*. Your production will be unique to you and your cast. That is the magic of live theater. What is interesting about these notes is that many of the performance details I mention were not part of the original stage directions. They either emerged spontaneously on performance day or were developed by students in rehearsal after the stage directions had been written into the script. My favorite pieces of stage business are the ones that arise directly from the students themselves, and demonstrate a union between actor and character, as if that individual becomes a vehicle for the character she is playing. To witness a fifteen-year-old girl "become" Bottom as Shakespeare's words leave her mouth is a memorable moment indeed.

SCENE 1 (ACT I, SCENE II)

As the production opens, New Age music plays on the boom box, and the fairies make their initial appearance, running onstage in glittering skirts, waving scarves and wands. They then huddle together, giggle loudly, and exit quickly. The introduction of the fairies at the beginning of the play sets the tone for the magic to follow. When the narrator recites the line about Puck's actions having "unexpected consequences," she should say it in a stage whisper, as if she is sharing a secret with the audience.

Puck's entrance should be skipping, playful, and graceful. After the line "straightaway loved an ass," Oberon and Puck perform an elaborate handshake involving high fives, hand slaps, and finger moves that culminates in an arms upraised "Woo!" These details, which should be worked out by the individual actors, go a long way toward establishing mood and relationships, in this case the playful and conspiratorial bond between Oberon and Puck. When Oberon asks Puck, "What hast thou done?" Puck retreats by walking backwards, making himself smaller and smaller by crouching. The relationship is playful, but clearly Oberon is the boss.

When the would-be lovers are anointed with flowers, the boom box operator should double as instrumentalist, and play a simple set of chimes at each anointment. These repeating sound cues reinforce the play's magical qualities, and provide an aural "motif" that audiences recognize and appreciate. A well-constructed production incorporates these repeating elements like a well-composed piece of music, and the structure gives the performance aesthetic unity.

There are a number of comedic touches student actors bring to this play. Lysander indulges in hysterical fake crying on "Look, when I vow I weep." Having bawled exaggeratedly for a few seconds, he pauses, glances to see if Helena is reacting, and when she turns to look at him, he begins to bawl again. The female characters also have their merry moments: On the line "O spite," Helena's arms are outstretched to the side, holding her two suitors apart, her hands on their foreheads as they swing their fists at each other. Then when she lets go, they crash into each other and collapse in a heap. On "Lysander's love," Lysander takes Hermia by the shoulders and turns her around facing the opposite direction, and he hastens toward Helena. The action on the stage physically illustrates the characters' emotional states: as the lover's eyes turn elsewhere, their bodies follow.

The competition between Lysander and Demetrius can likewise play itself out physically. When Lysander kneels at Helena's feet, Demetrius tries to kneel in the exact same spot. When Lysander tells Demetrius, "Withdraw, and prove it too," both actors turn and thumb-wrestle while on their knees, to riotous audience response. Hermia tries to break up the fight by separating their hands but she simply becomes entangled in the digital chaos.

Hermia physically illustrates her passionate desperation by hanging onto Lysander's leg as he walks, dragging her along the ground. When Lysander tells Hermia, "You bead, you acorn . . ." Hermia sits on the bench with her head in her hands, defeated and dejected. It is a touching stage picture especially following on the heels of her display of visible strength and passion.

As Demetrius and Lysander exit, they resume their thumb-wrestling match, which serves as a nice comic reprise. In retrospect, introducing the thumb wrestling a third time would have been wise, thus employing the ever-effective comedy rule of threes.

SCENE 2 (ACT IV, SCENE I)

When the narrator opens this scene with the words, "We are still in the woods," she looks around apprehensively, as if she is afraid of what might be lurking around her. This is a nice touch, and not only helps build a mood for the setting, but also makes the narrator part of the world we are creating. The actor playing Bottom in this production is very demanding and loud, similar to a diva—or Mick Jagger on tour. New Age music plays on the boom box as the glittery fairies dance about Bottom, who is enjoying his new status as a kind of deity.

In retrospect, I would have had this faerie dance last longer. Furthermore, I would have invited a dance choreographer from the school or from a local dance academy to guest design something fanciful. I hand out a questionnaire at the beginning of each project, asking students to list a few hobbies and interests. Those who mention dance are good candidates for movement-oriented roles. Their input is also valuable in choreography. Ideas and suggestions that come directly from the actors themselves are often the most valuable of all.

At the end Bottom's "dream" speech, he exits skipping. This was a choice by the actor playing Bottom, not mine as director. There is something so merry and innocent about the act of skipping. When Bottom skips offstage, he inspires the actors playing the two pairs of lovers to skip on for the following scene. It is almost as if the cast has imbibed a magical potion that causes them to skip. Even simple musical instruments or noisemakers played live by the actors themselves provide a lovely touch to any production. When the royalty enter to wake the sleeping lovers, the attendant uses a tambourine to wake them.

For this production of *A Midsummer Night's Dream,* cast members also add their own creative touches to the costuming, including a lovely "wall costume" for the character of Wall. Whenever young actors contribute creatively to a play, inspired performances follow.

SCENE 3 (ACT V, SCENE I)

Philostrate tells the Rude Mechanicals offstage that they have been chosen to perform, and a great cheer emerges from behind the curtain. Occasionally, offstage sounds are desirable. In this case, the whoops and hollers from the Rude Mechanicals set a merry tone for their performance and inform the audience of the personality of the group they are about to see.

The acting in the play within a play, *Pyramus and Thisbe,* offers actors a real opportunity to ham it up and exaggerate into ridiculousness. In other words, they can have fun! Wall has a nice rectangular cloth tunic with bricks painted on it that looks great when his arms are outstretched. On the line "Wicked Wall . . ." Bottom pushes Wall enthusiastically, as Wall, annoyed, pushes back. Wall's one line is spoken in such a sweet and quiet deadpan that the audience applauds when he exits. Even a quiet character can win over an audience with understated charm, and that is what Wall does in this production. Sometimes in acting, less is more, and Wall embodies that principle in this show. It is what he does not say and do that speaks volumes about his character.

Each actor in a production has something unique to offer audiences. The student playing Wall is a quiet and gentle person in real life, and when he speaks, he breathes that gentleness into his character and wins over the audience.

Moonshine enters dragging a stuffed dog on a leash. When he gets to the line "This dog is my dog," he shakes the leash and makes barking sounds, but he is not satisfied that this is adequate, so he reaches down and actually shakes the stuffed dog himself, inspiring audience laughter.

In this performance of *Pyramus and Thisbe,* each successive character is louder and more melodramatic than the previous one. When it comes to Lion's turn, he makes a huge roar and runs into the audience. He roars again, this time scaring himself with his own roar and running away offstage. As Pyramus, on the line "Come tears, confound," Bottom licks his finger and dabs his eyes elaborately with tears. Before dying, Bottom wipes off the surface of the stage with his shirtsleeve so that he can have a clean death spot. Mid-death, he stands up and takes a few bows to the audience and then continues dying. Finally, from a lying-down position, he sits up, takes one more bow, and dies again.

A small, wiry ninth grade boy, wearing a bright red wig, plays the character of Thisbe. As Thisbe falls, his wig flies off his head and lands a couple of feet away from him on the stage. Without missing a beat, he reaches out and grabs the wig, replaces it on his head, and dies again. These accidental comic moments are serendipitous, and if there are to be subsequent performances, they can be worked into the show permanently. As a bonus, audiences will probably continue to believe that they are spontaneous mishaps!

The final lines of the play ("If we shadows have offended . . .") are recited by the entire cast in unison. It is important for the actors to begin the lines while they are still gathering onstage so that the audience does not prematurely applaud. Simple choreography such as the group stepping left and right in unison can bring this merry and magical tale to a rousing finish. *A Midsummer Night's Dream* ranks as one of William Shakespeare's most colorful and lighthearted plays. Using this book as a guideline, I hope that the experience of performing this comedy will bring delight and laughter to both actors and audiences alike.

✳ *A MIDSUMMER NIGHT'S DREAM:*
SET AND PROP LIST

SET PIECES:

Two benches

PROPS:

SCENE 1:
Flower for Oberon
Chimes for magic sound effects
Scarves and Wands for fairies
SCENE 2:
Flower for Titania
Horn for sound effect
SCENE 3:
Paper for Philostrate
Sword for Pyramus and Thisbe
Mantle (handkerchief) for Thisbe
Tambourine to wake lovers
Stuffed dog, lantern, and leash for Moonshine

COSTUMES:

Ass head for Bottom. (Available online or can be constructed by an
    artistic student.)
Wall costume for Wall. Many possibilities, including a painted canvas.
Lion's head. Again, this can be purchased or constructed.
Wig for Thisbe

BENJAMIN BANNEKER ACADEMIC HIGH SCHOOL *presents*

A Midsummer Night's Dream
By William Shakespeare

Tuesday, April 11th, 2000
Instructor: David Ritzer | Guest Director: Nick Newlin

CAST OF CHARACTERS (IN ORDER OF APPEARANCE)

Narrator scene 1: Carrie Lambert
Oberon, king of the Fairies: Donald Williams
Robin Goodfellow (Puck), a hobgoblin in Oberon's service: Indira Hall
Hermia: Crystal M. Carter
Demetrius: Isaac Dua
Helena: Shante M. Hill
Lysander: Jeremy Drummond
Narrator Scene 2: Jennifer Dean
Titania, queen of the Fairies: Tonetta Brown
Nick Bottom the weaver/Pyramus: Maia Shanklin Roberts
Peasblossom: Rosalynne Jones
Cobweb: Tiffany Jackson
Mustardseed: Carrie Lambert
Theseus, duke of Athens: Michael Grady
Hippolyta, queen of the Amazons: Nakita Braboy
Egeus, father to Hermia: Son Tran
Narrator Scene 3: Kendra McDow
Philostrate, master of the revels to Theseus: Kristina Link
Peter Quince the carpenter/Prologue: Jennifer Dean
Tom Snout the tinker/Wall: Chauncey Moore
Francis Flute the bellows mender/Thisbe: Elobuike Oji
Snug the joiner/Lion: Chiwuba Ohan
Robin Starveling the tailor/Moon: Wendall Jefferson
Lords and Attendants on Theseus and Hippolyta: Eric Clark, Marcus A. Williams, Carlos Aviles
Fairies in the trains of Titania and Oberon: Kendra McDow, Kyla Allen, Currie Cheek

Stage Manager: Kendra McDow   **Programs:** Kyla Allen
Props: Eric Clark   **Costumes:** Currie Cheek
Sets: Marcus A. Williams   **Tech:** Carlos Aviles

Lord, what fools these mortals be!

ADDITIONAL RESOURCES

SHAKESPEARE

Shakespeare Set Free: Teaching Romeo and Juliet, Macbeth and a Midsummer Night's Dream
Peggy O'Brien, Ed., Teaching Shakespeare Institute
Washington Square Press
New York, 1993

Shakespeare Set Free: Teaching Hamlet and Henry IV, Part 1
Peggy O'Brien, Ed., Teaching Shakespeare Institute
Washington Square Press
New York, 1994

Shakespeare Set Free: Teaching Twelfth Night and Othello
Peggy O'Brien, Ed., Teaching Shakespeare Institute
Washington Square Press
New York, 1995

The *Shakespeare Set Free* series is an invaluable resource with lesson plans, activites, handouts, and excellent suggestions for rehearsing and performing Shakespeare plays in a classroom setting.

ShakesFear and How to Cure It!
Ralph Alan Cohen
Prestwick House, Inc.
Delaware, 2006

The Friendly Shakespeare: A Thoroughly Painless Guide to the Best of the Bard
Norrie Epstein
Penguin Books
New York, 1994

Brush Up Your Shakespeare!
Michael Macrone
Cader Books
New York, 1990

Shakespeare's Insults: Educating Your Wit
Wayne F. Hill and Cynthia J. Ottchen
Three Rivers Press
New York, 1991

Practical Approaches to Teaching Shakespeare
Peter Reynolds
Oxford University Press
New York, 1991

Scenes From Shakespeare:
A Workbook for Actors
Robin J. Holt
McFarland and Co.
London, 1988

101 Theatre Games for Drama
Teachers, Classroom Teachers
& Directors
Mila Johansen
Players Press Inc.
California, 1994

THEATER AND PERFORMANCE

Impro: Improvisation and the Theatre
Keith Johnstone
Routledge Books
London, 1982

A Dictionary of Theatre Anthropology:
The Secret Art of the Performer
Eugenio Barba and Nicola Savarese
Routledge
London, 1991

THEATER GAMES

Theatre Games for Young Performers
Maria C. Novelly
Meriwether Publishing
Colorado, 1990

Improvisation for the Theater
Viola Spolin
Northwestern University Press
Illinois, 1983

Theater Games for Rehearsal:
A Director's Handbook
Viola Spolin
Northwestern University Press
Illinois, 1985

PLAY DIRECTING

Theater and the Adolescent Actor:
Building a Successful School Program
Camille L. Poisson
Archon Books
Connecticut, 1994

Directing for the Theatre
W. David Sievers
Wm. C. Brown, Co.
Iowa, 1965

The Director's Vision: Play Direction
from Analysis to Production
Louis E. Catron
Mayfield Publishing Co.
California, 1989

INTERNET RESOURCES

http://www.folger.edu
The Folger Shakespeare Library's web site has lesson plans, primary sources, study guides, images, workshops, programs for teachers and students, and much more. The definitive Shakespeare website for educators, historians and all lovers of the Bard.

http://www.shakespeare.mit.edu.
*The Complete Works of
William Shakespeare.*
All complete scripts for *The
30-Minute Shakespeare* series were
originally downloaded from this site
before editing. Links to other internet
resources.

http://www.LoMonico.com/
Shakespeare-and-Media.htm
http://shakespeare-and-media
.wikispaces.com
Michael LoMonico is Senior
Consultant on National Education
for the Folger Shakespeare Library.
His *Seminar Shakespeare 2.0* offers a
wealth of information on how to use
exciting new approaches and online
resources for teaching Shakespeare.

http://www.freesound.org.
A collaborative database of sounds
and sound effects.

http://www.wordle.net.
A program for creating "word clouds"
from the text that you provide. The
clouds give greater prominence to
words that appear more frequently in
the source text.

http://www.opensourceshakespeare
.org.
This site has good searching capacity.

http://shakespeare.palomar.edu/
default.htm
Excellent links and searches

http://shakespeare.com/
Write like Shakespeare,
Poetry Machine, tag cloud

http://www.shakespeare-online.com/

http://www.bardweb.net/

http://www.rhymezone.com/
shakespeare/
Good searchable word and phrase
finder.
Or by lines:
http://www.rhymezone.com/
shakespeare/toplines/

http://shakespeare.mcgill.ca/
Shakespeare and Performance
research team

http://www.enotes.com/william-
shakespeare

Needless to say, the internet goes on and on with valuable Shakespeare resources.
The ones listed here are excellent starting points and will set you on your way in the
great adventure that is Shakespeare.

NICK NEWLIN has performed a comedy and variety act for international audiences for twenty-seven years. Since 1996, he has conducted an annual play directing residency affiliated with the Folger Shakespeare Library in Washington, D.C. Newlin received a BA with Honors from Harvard University in 1982 and an MA in Theater with an emphasis in Play Directing from the University of Maryland in 1996.

THE 30-MINUTE
SHAKESPEARE

A MIDSUMMER NIGHT'S DREAM
978-1-935550-00-6

ROMEO AND JULIET
978-1-935550-01-3

MUCH ADO ABOUT NOTHING
978-1-935550-03-7

MACBETH
978-1-935550-02-0

THE MERRY WIVES OF WINDSOR
978-1-935550-05-1

TWELFTH NIGHT
978-1-935550-04-4

AVAILABLE IN FALL 2010

AS YOU LIKE IT
978-1-935550-06-8

LOVE'S LABOR'S LOST
978-1-935550-07-5

THE COMEDY OF ERRORS
978-1-935550-08-2

KING LEAR
978-1-935550-09-9

HENRY IV, PART 1
978-1-935550-11-2

OTHELLO
978-1-935550-10-5

All plays $7.95, available in bookstores everywhere

"Nick Newlin's 30-minute play cuttings are perfect for students who have no experience with Shakespeare. Each 30-minute mini-play is a play in itself with a beginning, middle, and end." —Michael Ellis-Tolaydo, Department of Theater, Film, and Media Studies, St Mary's College of Maryland

PHOTOCOPYING AND PERFORMANCE RIGHTS